Food Chains in a
BACKYARD HABITAT

ISAAC NADEAU
Photographs by
DWIGHT KUHN

The Rosen Publishing Group's
PowerKids Press™
New York

To Janet and Lael, for sharing their backyard with me—Isaac Nadeau
To Brittney—Dwight Kuhn

Published in 2002 by The Rosen Publishing Group, Inc.
29 East 21st Street, New York, NY 10010

First Edition

Book Design: Emily Muschinske
Project Editor: Emily Raabe

All Photographs © Dwight Kuhn

Nadeau, Isaac.
    Food chains in a backyard habitat / Isaac Nadeau.— 1st ed.
        p. cm. — (The library of food chains and food webs)
    ISBN 0-8239-5759-4 (lib. bdg.)
  1. Urban ecology (Biology)—Juvenile literature. 2. Food chains (Ecology)—Juvenile literature. [1. Food chains (Ecology) 2. Ecology.]
  I. Title. II. Series.
    QH541.5.C6 N24 2002
577.5'616—dc21

00-012333

Manufactured in the United States of America

Contents

Where Are Food Chains?

All plants and animals need energy to survive. Plants such as strawberries get their energy from the sun. When a strawberry is eaten by an animal, such as a slug, some of the energy from the strawberry is passed on to the slug. If the slug is then eaten by a bird, energy is passed on again. A house cat might catch and eat the bird, and energy is passed on once more. The strawberries, the slug, the bird, and the cat are each a link in a food chain. Food chains show how plants and animals are connected by what they eat. They also show how plants and animals are connected by who eats them.

Where can you find a food chain? One of the places to see food chains is in your own backyard! If you don't have a backyard, you can look for food chains in action at a park or a playground. Look carefully. Sometimes the members of the food chain are very small.

Every member of a food chain depends on all the other members of that chain. If any part of the food chain is destroyed, the other parts of the chain all will be affected.

A Nice Place to Live

Almost everywhere you look, you can see plants and animals busy with their lives. Every creature needs a special place to live. There it can find food, shelter, water, and anything else it needs to make itself feel at home. This special place is called a habitat. Backyards can be part of people's habitats. People might grow food and flowers in backyards. They might use the backyard as a place to play, relax, and sometimes even cook. A backyard isn't just a good place for people to live, however. A backyard is a habitat for hundreds of other creatures, too.

Above: Some things in a backyard food chain, such as flowers and vegetables, were planted by people. Right: Other things, such as this potato beetle and this toad, come to the backyard because they can find good things to eat there.

Energy for Everyone

From where does energy come? It comes from the sun! All of the energy in backyard food chains comes from the sun. When a lettuce leaf collects energy from the sun, it uses much of that energy for its own growth. Some more of the energy is lost to the air as heat. The rest is stored in the plant's body. When a rabbit eats the lettuce, it uses this leftover energy. The energy that the rabbit doesn't use or lose as heat is all that remains for the animal, such as an owl, that eats the rabbit. By the time the owl comes along, most of the energy that came from the sun has been used. There are more rabbits than owls in backyards because there is more "rabbit food" than "owl food."

At each step in a food chain, the amount of energy changes. This creates a pattern called an energy pyramid. Each step on the pyramid has less energy than the one below it. The more times the energy from the sun is passed on, the less energy there is for the next step.

What do a blade of grass, a caterpillar, a robin, and a cat all have in common?

They all can be found in a backyard habitat, and they all need energy to live.

The Sun Collectors

The sun is where the food chain begins. Plants turn sunlight, air, and water into energy that can be used by living things. This is called **photosynthesis**. Plants are known as **producers** because they produce, or make, their own food from sunlight. Animals are known as **consumers**, because they eat producers and each other. A backyard garden is a good place to see photosynthesis. Lettuce, carrots, potatoes, and all of the other plants that people grow in gardens get their energy from the sun. When you eat a carrot from the garden, you are part of a food chain. When a chickadee eats seeds from a sunflower, it is part of a food chain. If there were not plants collecting energy from the sun, there would be no food chains in a backyard habitat.

The word photosynthesis comes from photo, for light, and synthesis, for change. When plants photosynthesize, they change sunlight into energy.

Backyard Herbivores

People are not the only ones who like to eat plants. Squirrels and caterpillars are two types of consumers that eat plants in the backyard. Consumers that only eat plants are called **herbivores**. Herbivores depend on plants for their survival. Can you think of other herbivores that might visit the backyard for a salad?

Producers and herbivores are two links in a food chain. There are more than just two links in a backyard food chain, however. Herbivores get their energy from plants, but they also pass energy on when they are eaten by other animals. This makes another link in our backyard food chain.

Sometimes plants depend on herbivores, too. When a caterpillar becomes a butterfly, for example, it feeds on the nectar of flowers. The butterfly helps the flowers reproduce by bringing pollen from one flower to another.

When a squirrel finishes eating an apple, it may carry a seed from the apple to another backyard. With luck, the seed will grow into a new apple tree.

Hunters in the Backyard

For many animals, the backyard is a dangerous place. This is because there are many **carnivores** in the backyard. Carnivores are consumers that eat only meat for food. Carnivores are the third link in the backyard food chain. Carnivores that hunt for their food are called predators. The animals that they hunt are called prey. One of the most feared of all backyard predators is the house cat. Its sharp claws, silent movements, and speed make it hard to escape. Cats often kill birds that live or nest in the backyard.

Carnivores that eat other carnivores are called secondary carnivores. Cats that eat birds are secondary carnivores. Secondary carnivores are the fourth link in a food chain, after producers, herbivores, and carnivores.

The praying mantis is a fierce backyard predator. It eats many different kinds of insects, even other praying mantises! This mantis is eating a grasshopper.

Garbage Duty

Eventually, everything that lives in the backyard dies. If it is not eaten by crows or other scavengers, it goes back to the soil. In the soil, millions of creatures called decomposers are waiting to gobble it up! Mushrooms are important decomposers.

Every neighborhood needs a clean-up crew. This is true in the backyard habitat, too. In many backyards, consumers called **omnivores** eat what other animals leave behind. Omnivores are consumers that will eat almost anything they find. They eat plants, animals, and even trash if they can get it. One of the most famous omnivores you can find in the backyard is the raccoon. Crows are also omnivores. Crows even eat the bodies of dead animals they find. Animals that find and eat dead animals are called **scavengers**. Because they eat many different kinds of things, omnivores and scavengers are part of many backyard food chains at the same time.

Besides eating from trash cans, raccoons eat nuts, berries, insects, eggs, mice, worms, frogs, and many other foods. Raccoons eat so much in the summer and fall that they can live all winter without eating a single thing!

The Soil is Alive!

Soil is more than just dirt. Soil is the home of all kinds of interesting creatures. These creatures have one of the most important jobs of all in food chains in a backyard habitat. They are called **decomposers** because they break down everything that dies in the backyard. This **decay** is important because it returns nutrients to the soil. Nutrients are the **vitamins**, **minerals**, and other things that living things need so they can grow and stay healthy. Plants use their roots to pull up nutrients from the soil. Without the decomposers, plants would not be able to live. Without the plants, nothing could live in the backyard! Most decomposers in the backyard are so small that you can only see them with a microscope. These decomposers are called bacteria. **Fungi**, such as mushrooms, are also decomposers. There are more bacteria in one backyard than there are people on Earth!

This peach is rotting with the help of bacteria and fungi.

One Big Backyard

Almost every living thing belongs to more than one food chain at the same time. When food chains connect, that is called a food web. These two pages show a backyard food web. The arrows point to the creature that is getting the energy. The mushrooms at the bottom right of the food web will help to decompose any creature that dies in the web.

Color Key

- carnivores
- decomposers
- herbivores
- omnivores
- producers

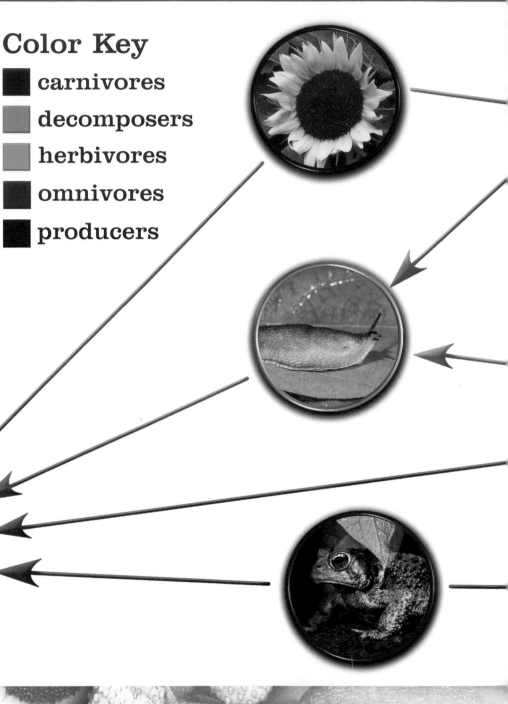

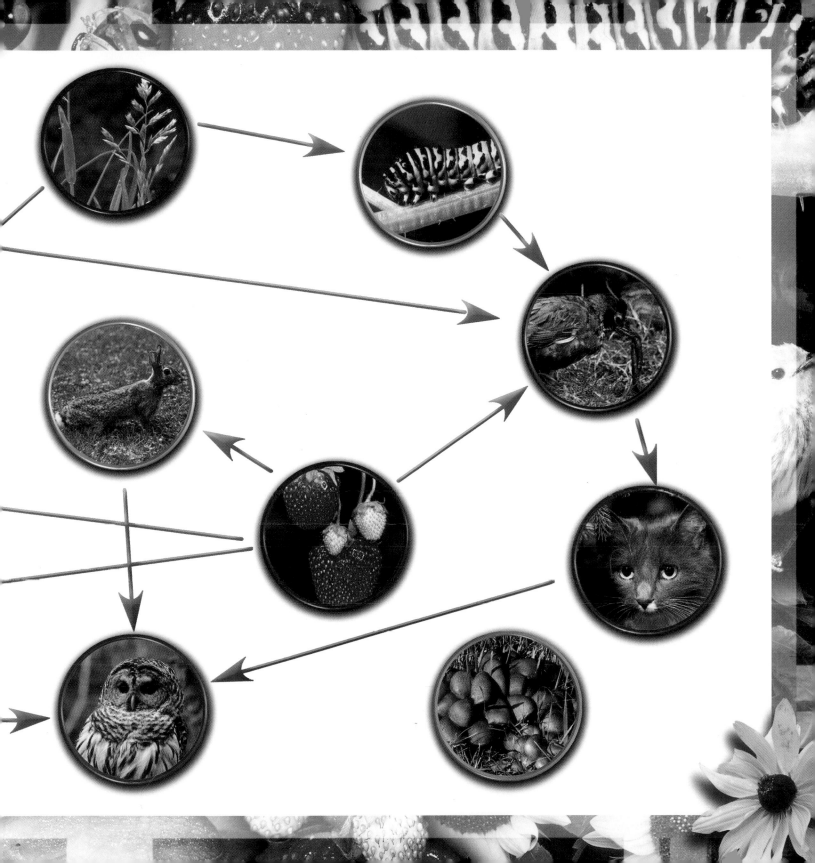

Exploring the Backyard Habitat

There are all kinds of ways to explore the world right in your own backyard, neighborhood park, or school playground. One good way to learn about food chains in the backyard is to plant something. Look closely when you dig in the soil. You will see all kinds of creatures living there. Wrap a bean in a wet paper towel. Keep it wet for a week. Has it begun to sprout? Now plant it in your backyard and watch it grow! Plant some sunflowers and see which animals like to eat the seeds. The more time you spend there, the more you will learn about the amazing world of food chains in a backyard habitat. In the early morning, you might see rabbits eating or a cat hunting in the backyard. If you go to the backyard just before dark, you might see a bat flying back and forth. It is probably hunting insects that fly. Even the air in the backyard is full of food chains!

Glossary

carnivores (KAR-nih-vorz) Animals that eat other animals for food.

consumers (con-SOO-merz) Animals that get their energy by eating producers and other animals. Herbivores, omnivores, carnivores, and scavengers are all consumers.

decay (dee-KAY) To rot.

decomposers (dee-cum-POH-zers) Living things that break down dead plants and animals into simpler parts.

fungi (FUN-geye) Members of a group of living things that feed off waste and dead things. They are like plants.

herbivores (ER-bih-vorz) Animals that eat plants.

minerals (MIH-ner-ulz) Natural ingredients from Earth's soil, such as iron or zinc, that are important parts of the food of living things.

omnivores (AHM-nih-vorz) Animals that eat both plants and animals.

photosynthesis (foh-toh-SIN-zthuh-sis) The process in which leaves use energy from sunlight, gases from air, and water from soil to make food and release oxygen.

producers (pruh-DOO-serz) Organisms that make their food from sunlight.

scavengers (SCAV-en-jerz) Animals that feed on dead animals.

vitamins (VY-tuh-minz) Nutrients that help the bodies of living things fight illness and grow strong.

Index

Web Sites

To learn more about backyard habitats, check out this Web site:
http://birdwebsite.com/backyard.htm
www.nwf.org/kids/other/wildl.html